Weekend Quilts & Pillows

Deborah Hearn

Each Project Pieced in 8 Hours or Less!

The Hearn's Popcorn

Chitra Publications

2 Public Avenue • Montrose, PA 18801-1220

Your Best Value in Quilting
www.QuiltTownUSA.com

Dedication: to the GOD of all comfort ... and my wonderful family! II Corinthians 1:2-3

Introduction

"What's your passion?" This is a question I was recently asked. One of the things I enjoy most is helping beginner quilters. Each year our community holds a "Quilt-in-a-Weekend" to encourage beginners, as well as more experienced quilters in their quilting and fellowship. I'm in charge of finding a pattern to suit both. For several months before the event, I start to look for a fast and easy pattern that everyone will enjoy. Since my goal is to have these quilters complete their quilt top during the weekend, it is always a challenge to come up with the perfect pattern.

Seeing a need for attractive quilts that are easy to make, I decided to design and stitch quilts that can be pieced in eight hours or less. You'll find these quilts great for beginners as well as more seasoned quilters who want a fast project to give as a gift, toss on a bed, or use in a family room. Each design comes with the added bonus of a pillow pattern that complements the quilt.

There's something for everyone on the following pages. So get ready to stitch. Whether it's your first quilt or your hundredth have fun and enjoy the results you achieve with *Weekend Quilts & Pillows!*

Deborah

Acknowledgment: *A special thank you to Terri Birchard for machine quilting the many quilts found in this book. Terri owns and operates T. L. C. Custom Quilting. To contact her, write to: Terri Birchard, T. L. C. Custom Quilting, 3205 Wayne Street, Endwell, New, York, 13760, or call her at (607)748-2781.*

Contents...

Homespun Square

Materials for the Quilt

- Fat eighth (11" x 18") light plaid
- 1/2 yard each of 12 assorted plaids
- 1 yard medium tan plaid
- 1 1/2 yards brown plaid
- 2 1/8 yards large black plaid
- 4 1/2 yards backing fabric
- 77" square of batting

Cutting for the Quilt

Cut lengthwise strips before cutting other pieces from the same yardage.
- Cut 1: 10 1/2" square, light print
- Cut 12: 5 1/2" squares, assorted plaids
- Cut 36: 5 1/2" x 13" strips, assorted plaids
- Cut 2: 5 1/2" x 30 1/2" lengthwise strips, medium tan plaid
- Cut 2: 5 1/2" x 20 1/2" lengthwise strips, medium tan plaid
- Cut 2: 5 1/2" x 50 1/2" lengthwise strips, brown plaid
- Cut 2: 5 1/2" x 40 1/2" strips, brown plaid
- Cut 2: 6 3/4" x 73" lengthwise strips, large black plaid
- Cut 2: 6 3/4" x 60 1/2" lengthwise strips, large black plaid

*I really like the look and feel of **"Homespun Square"** with its soft homespun fabrics that just beg to be curled up in. It's a perfect quilt to use indoors or out. The ragged edge adds to the relaxed look and makes finishing the quilt effortless.*

Directions

- Stitch two 5 1/2" plaid squares together. Make 2.
- Stitch them to opposite sides of the 10 1/2" light print square.
- Stitch four 5 1/2" plaid squares together. Make 2.
- Stitch them to the remaining sides of the unit, as shown.

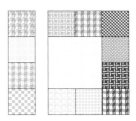

- Stitch the 5 1/2" x 20 1/2" medium tan plaid strips to opposite sides of the quilt.
- Stitch the 5 1/2" x 30 1/2" medium tan plaid strips to the remaining sides of the quilt.
- Stitch six 5 1/2" x 13" plaid strips together, along their length, to make a pieced panel.
- Cut two 5 1/2" slices from the pieced panel. Stitch them to opposite sides of the quilt, reversing their order.

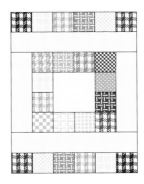

- Stitch eight 5 1/2" x 13" plaid strips together to make a pieced panel.
- Cut two 5 1/2" slices from the pieced panel.
- Stitch them to opposite sides of the quilt, reversing their order, as shown.

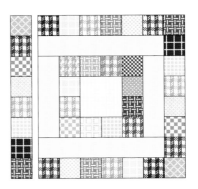

- Stitch the 5 1/2" x 40 1/2" brown plaid strips to opposite sides of the quilt.
- Stitch the 5 1/2" x 50 1/2" brown plaid strips to the remaining sides of the quilt.
- Stitch ten 5 1/2" x 13" plaid strips together to make a pieced panel.
- Cut two 5 1/2" slices from the pieced panel. Stitch them to opposite sides of the quilt, reversing their order.
- Stitch twelve 5 1/2" x 13" plaid strips together to make a pieced panel.
- Cut two 5 1/2" slices from the pieced panel. Stitch them to opposite sides of the quilt, reversing their order.
- Stitch the 6 3/4" x 60 1/2" large black plaid strips to opposite sides of the quilt.
- Stitch the 6 3/4" x 73" large black plaid strips to the remaining sides of the quilt.
- Layer the quilt in this manner: backing right side down, batting, and quilt top, right side up.
- Quilt as desired, stopping 1 1/8" from the outer edge.
- Stitch a 1 1/8" seam allowance around the outside edges of the quilt.
- Trim the batting close to the stitching line and trim the backing even with the quilt top.
- Clip into the seam allowance around the outside edge every 3/4" almost to the stitching. Dampen the edge of the quilt to make the edges curl when dry.

Size: 18" square

Homespun Pillow

Directions

- Stitch the nine 4" plaid squares into 3 rows of 3, with the light plaid square in the center.
- Stitch the 1 1/2" x 11" medium tan plaid strips to opposite sides of the pillow top.
- Stitch the 1 1/2" x 13" medium tan plaid strips to the remaining sides of the pillow top.
- Stitch the 3 3/4" x 13" small black plaid strips to opposite sides of the pillow top.
- Stitch the 3 3/4" x 19 1/2" small black plaid strips to the remaining sides of the pillow top.
- Layer in this manner: muslin, batting and pillow top, right side up. Quilt as desired, stopping 1 1/8" from the outer edge.
- Center the pillow top on the 20" square of backing, right sides out, and stitch with a 1 1/8" seam allowance around the outside edges of the pillow top, leaving a 10" opening on one side.
- Insert the pillow form. Finish stitching the opening closed.
- Trim the batting close to the stitching line and trim the backing even with the pillow top.
- Clip into the seam allowance around the outside edge every 3/4" almost to the stitching. Dampen the edge of the pillow top to make the edges curl when dry.

Materials for the Pillow

- Eight 4" assorted dark plaid squares
- One 4" light plaid square
- 1/8 yard medium tan plaid
- 1/4 yard small black plaid
- 20" square of muslin
- 20" square of backing fabric
- 20" square of batting
- 18" square pillow form

Cutting for the Pillow

- Cut 2: 1 1/2" x 11" strips, medium tan plaid
- Cut 2: 1 1/2" x 13" strips, medium tan plaid
- Cut 2: 3 3/4" x 13" strips, small black plaid
- Cut 2: 3 3/4" x 19 1/2" strips, small black plaid

Patched Fence

The traditional Nine Patch and Rail Fence blocks team up to create a graphic design. Stitch your own *"Patched Fence"* using a combination of your favorite complementary fabrics. Just be sure one is light and the other is dark.

Patched Fence

Materials for the Quilt

- 5 yards blue print
- 3 yards tan with blue stripe
- 4 1/2 yards backing fabric
- 80" square of batting

Cutting for the Quilt

Cut the lengthwise strips before cutting other pieces from the same yardage.
- Cut 2: 5 1/2" x 68" lengthwise strips, blue print
- Cut 2: 5 1/2" x 78" lengthwise strips, blue print
- Cut 36: 2 1/2" x 44" crosswise strips, blue print
- Cut 38: 2 1/2" x 44" crosswise strips, tan with blue stripe. You will use 8 for the binding.

Directions

- Stitch a 2 1/2" x 44" blue print strip between two 2 1/2" x 44" tan stripe strips to make a panel, as shown. Make 8.
- Cut one hundred and twenty-two 2 1/2" slices from the panels to make strip A.

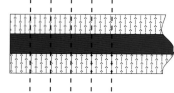

- Stitch a 2 1/2" x 44" tan stripe strip between two 2 1/2" x 44" blue print strips to make a panel. Make 14. Set aside 10 panels for the Rail Fence blocks.
- Cut sixty-one 2 1/2" slices from the remaining panels to make strip B.
- Stitch a strip B between two strip A's to make a Nine Patch block, as shown. Make 61.

- Cut sixty 6 1/2" slices from the set-aside panels for the Rail Fence blocks, as shown.

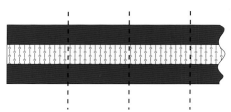

Assembly

- Lay out the blocks in 11 rows of 11 making sure the stripes in the Nine Patches run in the same direction.

- Stitch the blocks into rows. Join the rows.
- Measure the length of the quilt. Trim the 5 1/2" x 68" blue print strips to that measurement and stitch them to opposite sides of the quilt.
- Measure the width of the quilt, including the borders. Trim the 5 1/2" x 78" blue print strips to that measurement and stitch them to the remaining sides of the quilt.
- Finish the quilt according to the *General Directions* using the remaining 2 1/2" x 44" tan stripe strips for the binding.

Patched Fence Pillow

Materials for the Pillow

- 5/8 yard blue print
- 1/4 yard tan with blue stripe
- 24" square of muslin
- 24" square of backing fabric
- 24" square of batting
- 18" square pillow form
- Two 1 1/8" flat cover buttons
- Heavyweight thread

Cutting for the Pillow

- Cut 2: 2 1/2" x 44" strips, blue print
- Cut 1: 2 1/2" x 28" strip, blue print
- Cut 2: 2 1/2" x 18 1/2" strips, blue print, for the border
- Cut 2: 2 1/2" x 22 1/2" strips, blue print, for the border
- Cut 1: 2 1/2" x 44" crosswise strip, tan with blue stripe
- Cut 2: 2 1/2" x 28" crosswise strips, tan with blue stripe

Directions

- Stitch a 2 1/2" x 44" tan stripe strip between two 2 1/2" x 44" blue print strips to make a panel.
- Cut five 2 1/2" slices from the panel and label them A; and cut four 6 1/2" slices for the Rail Fence blocks.
- Stitch a 2 1/2" x 28" blue print strip between two 2 1/2" x 28" tan stripe strips to make a panel.
- Cut ten 2 1/2" slices from the panel and label them B.
- Stitch an A between 2 B's to make a Nine Patch block. Make 5.

Assembly

- Referring to the pillow photo, lay out the Nine Patch blocks and the Rail Fence blocks in 3 rows of 3.
- Stitch the blocks into rows. Join the rows.
- Stitch the 2 1/2" x 18 1/2" blue print strips to opposite sides of the pillow top.
- Stitch the 2 1/2" x 22 1/2" blue print strips to the remaining sides of the pillow top.
- Layer in this manner: muslin, batting, and pillow top, right side up, and quilt as desired.
- Center the pillow top on the backing fabric, right sides together. Stitch a 1/4" seam allowance around the outside edge of the pillow top, leaving a 12" opening.
- Trim the muslin, batting, and backing even with the pillow top.
- Turn the pillow top right side out.
- Stitch in the ditch along the inside edge of the blue border, leaving a 12" opening on the same side as before.
- Insert the pillow form.
- Continue stitching the inner opening closed.
- Blindstitch the outer opening closed.
- Cover the 2 buttons with blue print fabric, following the manufacturer's directions.
- Using the heavyweight thread, attach one button to the center of each side of the pillow, pulling the thread tight.

Garden Rickrack

Looking for a way to display lots of pastel prints? *"Garden Rickrack"* has the perfect palette to achieve a soft-looking quilt. The long winter days in Northeast Pennsylvania will seem less harsh now that an indoor summer garden will be spread across a bed.

Materials for the Quilt

- Assorted print scraps at least 2" square and totaling at least 3/4 yard
- 1/8 yard each of yellow, pale blue, pink, and purple print
- 1 1/2 yards light print
- 1 1/2 yards backing fabric
- 41" x 54" piece of batting

Cutting for the Quilt

- Cut 216: 2" squares, assorted small prints
- Cut 15: 5" squares, light print
- Cut 4: 7 3/4" squares, light print, then cut them in quarters diagonally to yield 16 setting triangles
- Cut 2: 4 1/4" squares, light print, then cut them in half diagonally to yield 4 corner triangles
- Cut 2: 5 1/2" x 44" strips, light print
- Cut 2: 5 1/2" x 39" strips, light print
- Cut 5: 2 1/2" x 44" strips, light print, for the binding
- Cut 1: 1 1/4" x 40" strip, yellow print
- Cut 1: 1 1/4" x 40" strip, pale blue print
- Cut 1: 1 1/4" x 28" strip, pink print
- Cut 1: 1 1/4" x 28" strip, purple print

Directions

For the Nine Patch blocks:

- Stitch three 2" print squares together, as shown. Make 72 pieced strips.
- Stitch 3 pieced strips together to make a Nine Patch block. Make 24.

Assembly

- Lay out the Nine Patch blocks, the 5" light print squares, setting triangles, and corner triangles, as shown.

- Stitch the squares and triangles into diagonal rows. Join the rows.
- Measure the length of the quilt. Trim the 1 1/4" x 40" yellow print and pale blue print strips to that measurement. Stitch them to the long sides of the quilt.
- Measure the width of the quilt, including the borders. Trim the 1 1/4" x 28" pink print and purple print strips to that measurement. Stitch them to the remaining sides of the quilt.
- In the same manner, trim the 5 1/2" x 44" light print strips to fit the quilt's length and stitch them to the long sides of the quilt.
- Trim the 5 1/2" x 39" light print strips to fit the quilt's width and stitch them to the remaining sides of the quilt.
- Finish the quilt according to the *General Directions*, using the 2 1/2" x 44" light print strips for the binding.

"Patches the Dog" Pillow

Materials for the Pillow

- Assorted print scraps at least 2" square and totaling at least 5/8 yard
- Four 2" squares brown print for the nose
- Two 2" squares, each with a 1/2" diameter dot centered in the square, for the eyes
- 1/8 yard light print
- Two 16" squares of batting
- Fiberfill

Cutting for the Pillow

- Cut 162: 2" squares, assorted prints
- Cut 3: A, light print, lining, for the ears and tail (pattern on page 25)

Directions

- Arrange a dog shape with fifty-two 2" print squares, one 2" brown print square, and one 2" square with the dot, as shown.

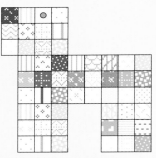

- Stitch the squares into vertical rows, starting and stopping at the 1/4" seam allowance on all outside and inside corners.
- In the same manner, lay out and stitch fifty-two 2" print squares, one 2" brown print square, and one 2" square with the dot, to create a reversed image of the dog's body. Set them aside.
- Lay out six 2" print squares in 3 rows of 2 to make a 6-patch unit. Make 3.
- Zigzag over all the seamlines of the 6-patch units.
- Center a lining A on a 6-patch unit, right sides

together.

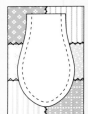

- Stitch around the edge of the lining with a 1/4" seam allowance leaving the straight edge open and backstitching at the beginning and end.
- Trim the 6-patch unit even with the edge of the lining and clip into the seam allowance on the curved edge. Make 3.
- Turn the ears and tail right side out through the opening.
- Make a continuous row of forty-two 2" print squares, placing the 2" brown print squares in the 3rd and 4th positions, and stitching the tail between the 15th and 16th square to make a 42-patch unit, as shown. Set it aside.

- Place each body section on a 16" square of batting.
- Zigzag over all of the seamlines of the patches on each body section and the 42-patch unit. Trim the batting even with the dog.
- Referring to the pillow photo for placement, baste an ear to each section, stitching in the seam allowance.
- Starting at the dog's chin on the body section, stitch the chain of patches to the dog shape, right sides together, matching the intersections of the squares. Pivot at the corners.
- Join the ends of the 42-patch unit before stitching completely around the body of the dog.
- In the same manner, stitch the opposite side of the 42-patch section to the remaining body section, leaving a 3" opening in the tummy area.
- Stuff the dog with fiberfill. Blindstitch the opening closed.

Big Sister Quilt

When a new baby arrives, the big sister or brother may feel a little left out. Sew this *"Big Sister Quilt"* (a variation of *"Baby Quilt"* on page 16) to make a little someone feel special. It's fast, easy and sure to be enjoyed since their favorite blankie is probably well worn.

19

Big Sister Quilt

Materials for the Quilt

- Assorted print scraps, each at least 2 1/2" square and totaling at least 1 1/8 yards
- 1 3/4 yards each of yellow, pale blue, pink, and purple prints NOTE: *If you prefer to piece the vertical strips to save fabric, you will need 1/3 yard of each fabric.*
- 1 1/2 yards light print
- 1 3/4 yards backing fabric
- 44" x 64" piece of batting

Cutting for the Quilt

- Cut 189: 2 1/2" squares, assorted prints
- Cut 4: 4" x 63" strips, one each of yellow, pale blue, pink, and purple prints; or cut two 4" x 32" strips of each color for pieced sashing strips
- Cut 9: 9 3/4" squares, light print, then cut them in quarters diagonally to yield 36 setting triangles
- Cut 6: 5 1/8" squares, light print, then cut them in half diagonally to yield 12 corner triangles
- Cut 6: 2 1/2" x 44" strips, light print, for the binding

Directions

For the Nine Patch blocks:
- Stitch three 2 1/2" print squares together to make a pieced strip, as shown. Make 63.

- Stitch 3 pieced strips together to make a Nine Patch block. Make 21.

Assembly

- Lay out 7 Nine Patch blocks on point with 12 setting triangles and 4 corner triangles in a vertical row. Stitch the blocks and triangles into diagonal rows. Join the rows. Make 3.

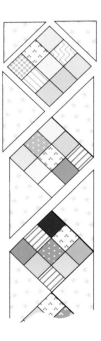

- NOTE: *To piece your vertical sashing strips, stitch two 4" x 32" same print strips together, end to end. Make 4.*
- Measure the length of the pieced rows. Trim the 4" x 63" strips to that measurement.
- Referring to the quilt photo for placement, stitch the pieced rows between the sashing strips.
- Finish the quilt according to the *General Directions* using the 2 1/2" x 44" light print strips for the binding.

My Quilted Heart Pillow

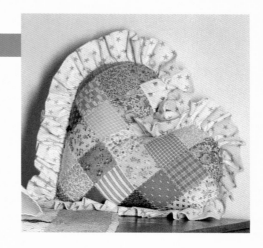

Materials for the Pillow

- Assorted print scraps each at least 2 1/2" square and totaling at least 1/2 yard
- 1/3 yard light print
- 14" square of backing fabric
- 14" square of batting
- Fiberfill
- 11" x 14" piece of paper

Cutting for the Pillow

- Cut 49: 2 1/2" squares, assorted prints
- Cut 2: 4 1/2" x 44" strips, light print, for the ruffle

Directions

- Lay out the forty-nine 2 1/2" print squares in 7 rows of 7.
- Stitch the squares into rows. Join the rows to make a patchwork square.
- Place the patchwork square on top of the 14" square of batting.
- Zigzag stitch over all the seams of the squares.
- Fold the paper in half so that it measures 7" x 11". Place a 6" plate on top of the paper aligning the edges with the fold and draw a semi-circle, then extend the line diagonally to the bottom left corner of the paper, as shown.

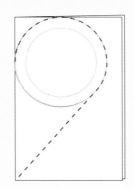

- Cut on the drawn line to make a heart pattern.
- Open the paper and modify it, if desired. Place the heart pattern on top of the quilted patchwork square. Trace around the outside edge of the pattern.
- Cut on the drawn line.
- Stitch the two 4 1/2" x 44" light print strips together, end to end, to make a long strip.
- Fold both ends of the long strip under 1/2", wrong side in, and press. Fold the long strip in half lengthwise, wrong side in and press.
- Baste 2 lines of stitching, one at 1/8" and one at 3/8" from the raw edge. Pull the 2 underneath threads to gather the ruffle.
- Place the ends of the ruffle at the inner point of the heart overlapping the ends at the 1/4" seamline. Evenly space the gathers and pin the ruffle to the heart, aligning the raw edges.

- Baste the ruffle to the pillow top.
- Stitch the pillow top and ruffle to the backing, right sides together, leaving a 6" opening on one of the straight sides of the pillow top.
- Trim the backing along the edge of the pillow top. Clip into the seam allowance along the curves, as necessary, and turn the pillow top, right side out.
- Stuff with fiberfill and blindstitch the opening closed.

Checkers Anyone?

Materials for the Quilt

- 2 yards gold print
- 3 1/8 yards blue print
- 3 1/4 yards red print or stripe
- 4 1/2 yards backing fabric
- 82" square of batting

Cutting for the Quilt

Cut lengthwise strips before cutting other pieces from the same yardage.

For the checkerboard:
- Cut 8: 6 1/2" x 28" strips, gold print
- Cut 8: 6 1/2" x 28" strips, blue print

For the 6 Star blocks:
- Cut 24: 3 1/2" x 6 1/2" rectangles, red print or stripe
- Cut 24: 3 1/2" squares, red print or stripe
- Cut 6: 6 1/2" squares, gold print
- Cut 48: 3 1/2" squares, gold print

Also:
- Cut 6: 3 1/2" x 56" lengthwise strips, blue print
- Cut 4: 3 1/2" x 23" strips, blue print
- Cut 4: 5" x 56" lengthwise strips, red print or stripe
- Cut 6: 2 1/2" x 56" lengthwise strips, red print or stripe, for the binding
- Cut 8: 5" x 23" strips, red print or stripe

*How happy I am that my daughter, Ann Baxter, loves to quilt too! She found that piecing **"Checkers Anyone?"** was so easy. The stars and stripes surrounding the quilt center make a perfect frame for this large checkerboard.*

Directions

For the quilt center:
- Stitch two 6 1/2" x 28" gold print strips and two 6 1/2" x 28" blue print strips together, along their length, alternating colors to make a pieced panel. Make 4.
- Cut four 6 1/2" sections from each panel, as shown.

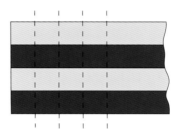

- Stitch 2 sections together, alternating direction, to make a unit, as shown. Make 8.

- Stitch 4 units together to make a pieced section, as shown. Make 2.

- Stitch the 2 pieced sections together to complete the checkerboard.
- Measure the length of the checkerboard. Trim 2 of the 3 1/2" x 56" blue print strips to that measurement and stitch them to opposite sides of the checkerboard.
- Measure the width of the checkerboard, including the borders. Trim two of the 3 1/2" x 56" blue print strips to that measurement and stitch them to the remaining sides of the checkerboard.

For the Star blocks:

• Draw a diagonal line from corner to corner on the wrong side of each 3 1/2" gold print square.

• Place a marked square on a 3 1/2" x 6 1/2" red print or stripe rectangle, right sides together. Stitch on the drawn line, as shown.

• Press the gold print square toward the corner, aligning the edges. Trim 1/4" beyond the stitching.

• In the same manner, place a gold print square on the opposite end of the red print or stripe rectangle. Stitch on the marked line. Press and trim as before, to make a pieced rectangle. Make 24.

• Lay out a 6 1/2" gold print square, 4 pieced rectangles, and four 3 1/2" red print or stripe squares. Stitch

them into rows and join the rows to make a Star block, as shown. Make 6.

• Stitch a 3 1/2" x 23" blue print strip between two 5" x 23" red print or stripe strips along their length to make a short pieced border. Make 4.

• Stitch a Star block between two short pieced borders.

• Measure the width of the quilt. Trim the short

Checkers Anyone? Pillow

Size: 19" x 22"

Materials for the Pillow

• 1/4 yard gold print
• 1/3 yard blue print
• 3/4 yard red print or stripe
• 21" x 24" piece of muslin
• 21" x 24" piece of backing fabric
• 21" x 24" piece of batting
• 14" square pillow form
• Eight 1 1/4" buttons, 4 red and 4 blue

Cutting for the Pillow

• Cut 7: 2 1/2" x 12" strips, gold print
• Cut 7: 2 1/2" x 12" strips, blue print
• Cut 2: 1" x 14 1/2" strips, blue print, for the inner border
• Cut 2: 1" x 15 1/2" strips, blue print, for the inner border
• Cut 2: 2 1/2" x 15 1/2" strips, red print or stripe, for the outer border
• Cut 2: 4" x 19 1/2" strips, red print or stripe, for the outer border

Directions

• Stitch four 2 1/2" x 12" blue print strips and three 2 1/2" x 12" gold print strips together, along their length, alternating colors to make a pieced panel.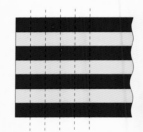
• Cut four 2 1/2" slices from the pieced panel.
• In the same manner, stitch three 2 1/2" x 12" blue print strips and four 2 1/2" x 12" gold print strips together and cut three 2 1/2" slices from the pieced panel.
• Referring to the pillow photo, lay out the strips in 7 rows. Join the rows.
• Stitch the 1" x 14 1/2" blue print strips to opposite sides of the pillow top.
• Stitch the 1" x 15 1/2" blue print strips to the remaining sides of the pillow top.
• Stitch the 2 1/2" x 15 1/2" red print or stripe strips to opposite sides of the pillow top.
• Stitch the 4" x 19 1/2" red print or stripe strips to the remaining sides of the pillow top.
• Layer in this manner: muslin, batting, and quilt top, right side up, and quilt as desired.

pieced borders to that measurement, trimming evenly from each end to keep the Star block centered.

• Stitch the trimmed Star section between two Star blocks to make a long pieced border. Make 2. Set them aside.

• Stitch a 3 1/2" x 56" blue print strip between two 5" x 56" red print or stripe strips along their length to make a pieced border. Make 2.

• Measure the length of the quilt. Trim the pieced borders to that measurement and stitch them to opposite sides of the quilt.

• Stitch the long pieced borders to the remaining sides.

• Finish the quilt according to the *General Directions*, using the 2 1/2" x 56" red print or stripe strips for the binding.

• Center the pillow top on the backing fabric, right sides together.

• Stitch around the outside edge of the pillow top, leaving a 10" opening.

• Trim the batting, muslin, and backing even with the pillow top.

• Turn the pillow top right side out.

• Stitch in the ditch along the outer edge of the blue border, leaving a 10" opening on the same side as before.

• Insert the pillow form.

• Stitch in the ditch along the remaining outer edge of the blue print border.

• Blindstitch the outer seam of the pillow closed.

• Center and attach the red buttons to one wide border and blue buttons to the other.

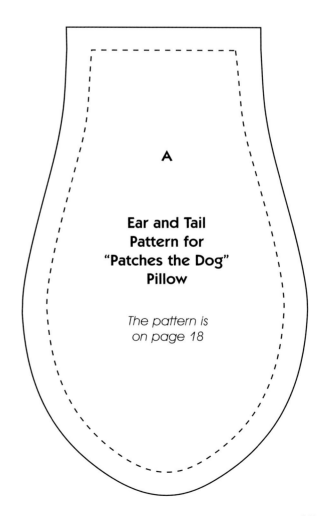

A

Ear and Tail Pattern for "Patches the Dog" Pillow

The pattern is on page 18

All American

Do you want to make a fun quilt? **"All American"** is as easy as apple pie and cute, too, when placed on a bed or hung on a wall. The long stripes and bright stars shout out, "made in the U.S.A!"

Materials for the Quilt

- 1 1/2 yards blue print
- 2/3 yards gold print
- 3 yards red print
- 2 1/3 yards tan print
- 6 yards backing fabric
- 64" x 104" piece of batting

Cutting for the Quilt

Cut lengthwise strips before cutting other pieces from the same yardage.

For the 5 Stars:
- Cut 20: 3 1/2" squares, blue print
- Cut 20: 3 1/2" x 6 1/2" rectangles, blue print
- Cut 5: 6 1/2" squares, gold print
- Cut 40: 3 1/2" squares, gold print

For the Stripes:
- Cut 6: 6" x 74" lengthwise strips, red print
- Cut 5: 6" x 74" lengthwise strips, tan print
- Cut 1: 6" x 61" lengthwise strip, tan print

Also:
- Cut 5: 12 1/2" squares, blue print
- Cut 9: 2 1/2" x 44" strips, red print, for the binding

Directions

For the Star blocks:
- Draw a diagonal line from corner to corner on the wrong side of each 3 1/2" gold print square.
- Place a marked gold print square on a 3 1/2" x 6 1/2" blue print rectangle, right sides together. Stitch on the drawn line, as shown.
- Press the gold print square toward the corner,

aligning the edges. Trim the seam allowance to 1/4" beyond the stitching.
- In the same manner, place a marked gold print square on the opposite end of the blue print rectangle. Stitch on the marked line. Press and trim, as before, to make a pieced rectangle. Make 20.
- Lay out the pieced rectangles, 6 1/2" gold print square, and the 3 1/2" blue print squares. Stitch them into rows and join the rows to complete a Star block. Make 5.

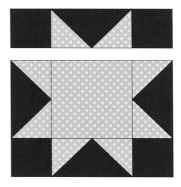

Assembly
- Referring to the quilt photo on the back cover, lay out the Star blocks and 12 1/2" blue print squares in 2 rows of 5.
- Stitch the blocks and squares into rows. Join the rows to complete the star section of the quilt. Set it aside.

For the Stripes:
- Stitch a 6" x 74" red print strip and a 6" x 74" tan print strip, right sides together along their length to make a pieced strip. Make 5.
- Stitch the pieced strips together, along their length. Stitch the remaining 6" x 74" red print strip to the tan print side to complete the stripe panel.
- Measure one long side of the star section. Trim the 6" x 61" tan print strip to that measurement.
- Using the same measurement, adjust the seams on the stripe panel, if needed, to fit the width of the star section.
- Stitch the trimmed tan print strip between the star section and the stripe panel to complete the quilt top.
- Finish the quilt according to the *General Directions*, using the 2 1/2" x 44" red print strips for the binding.

All Star Pillow

Materials for the Pillow

- 1/4 yard gold print
- 3/4 yard blue print
- 1/4 yard red print
- 1/4 yard tan print
- 25" square of muslin
- 25" square of backing fabric
- 25" square of batting
- 18" square pillow form
- Red Star button
- 20" of thin jute

Cutting for the Pillow

For the Star:
- Cut 1: 6 1/2" square, gold print
- Cut 8: 3 1/2" squares, gold print
- Cut 4: 3 1/2" x 6 1/2" rectangles, blue print
- Cut 4: 3 1/2" squares, blue print

Also:
- Cut 4: 1 1/2" x 32" strips, red print
- Cut 1: 1 1/2" x 15" strip, red print
- Cut 2: 1 1/2" x 32" strips, tan print
- Cut 2: 1 1/2" x 15" strips, tan print
- Cut 2: 3" x 18 1/2" strips, blue print
- Cut 2: 3" x 23 1/2" strips, blue print

Directions

- Make a Star block following the directions in the quilt pattern.
- Stitch a 1 1/2" x 32" tan print strip between two 1 1/2" x 32" red print strips to make a panel. Make 2.
- Cut two 12 1/2" slices and two 1 1/2" slices from each pieced panel. Label the 1 1/2" slices A.

- Stitch a 1 1/2" x 15" red print strip between two 1 1/2" x 15" tan print strips to make a panel.
- Cut eight 1 1/2" slices from the panel and label them B.
- Stitch an A slice between 2 B slices to make a Nine Patch, as shown. Make 4.
- Stitch 12 1/2" slices to 2 opposite sides of the Star block.
- Stitch a 12 1/2" slice between 2 Nine Patch blocks to make a pieced border. Make 2. Stitch the pieced borders to the remaining sides of the Star block.
- Stitch the 3" x 18 1/2" blue print strips to opposite sides of the pillow center.
- Stitch the 3" x 23 1/2" blue print strips to the remaining sides.
- Layer in this manner: muslin, batting and pillow top, right side up. Quilt as desired.
- Center the pillow top on the backing fabric, right sides together.
- Stitch around the outside edge of the pillow top, leaving a 10" opening.
- Trim the batting, muslin, and backing even with the pillow top.
- Turn the pillow top right side out.
- Stitch in the ditch along the outer edge of the striped border, leaving a 10" opening on the same side as before.
- Insert the pillow form.
- Stitch in the ditch along the remaining outer edge of the striped border.
- Blindstitch the outer seam of the pillow closed.
- Attach the red star button with jute in the center of the pillow, stitching through to the back of the pillow. Tie the jute into a bow.

daughter-in-law, Kelley Hearn, loves to
w and is always dreaming of her next
ilt. Kelley stitched *"The Village Green"*
ing the Puss-in-the-Corner block design.
e pieced squares create a delicate chain
at softly flows throughout the quilt.

*The
Village
Green*

The Village Green

Materials for the Quilt

- 2 1/2 yards green print
- 3 3/4 yards yellow print
- 2/3 yard green plaid
- 4 1/2 yards backing fabric
- 69" x 84" piece of batting

Cutting for the Quilt

Cut lengthwise strips before cutting other pieces from the same yardage.

- Cut 2: 4 1/4" x 67" lengthwise strips, green print
- Cut 2: 4 1/4" x 52" lengthwise strips, green print
- Cut 4: 4 1/4" x 44" strips, green print
- Cut 8: 2 1/4" x 44" strips, green print
- Cut 4: 2 1/4" x 67" lengthwise strips, yellow print
- Cut 4: 2 1/4" x 52" lengthwise strips, yellow print
- Cut 8: 2 1/4" x 44" strips, yellow print
- Cut 4: 4 1/4" x 44" strips, yellow print
- Cut 31: 7 3/4" squares, yellow print
- Cut 8: 2 1/2" x 44" green plaid strips, for the binding

Directions

- Stitch a 4 1/4" x 44" green print strip between two 2 1/4" x 44" yellow print strips to make a panel. Make 4.

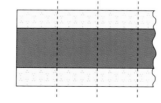

- Cut thirty-six 4 1/4" slices from the panels to make unit A's, as shown.
- Stitch a 4 1/4" x 44" yellow print strip between two 2 1/4" x 44" green print strips to make a panel. Make 4.
- Cut seventy-two 2 1/4" slices from the panels to make unit B's.

- Stitch a unit A between 2 unit B's to make a Puss-in-the-Corner block, as shown. Make 36.
- Lay out 32 Puss-in-the-Corner blocks and the 7 3/4" yellow print squares in 9 rows of 7, as shown.

- Stitch the blocks into rows. Join the rows.
- Stitch a 4 1/4" x 67" green print strip between two 2 1/4" x 67" yellow print strips to make a long pieced border. Make 2.
- Measure the length of the quilt. Trim the long pieced borders to that measurement. Set them aside.
- Stitch a 4 1/4" x 52" green print strip between two 2 1/4" x 52" yellow print strips to make a short pieced border. Make 2.
- Measure the width of the quilt. Trim the short pieced borders to that measurement.
- Stitch a short pieced border between 2 Puss-in-the-Corner blocks. Make 2.
- Stitch the long pieced borders to the long sides of the quilt.
- Stitch the short pieced borders to the remaining sides of the quilt.
- Finish the quilt according to the *General Directions*, using the 2 1/2" x 44" green plaid strips for the binding.

Village Green Pillow

Materials for the Pillow

- 1/4 yard green print
- 1 1/3 yards yellow print
- 1 1/4 yards muslin (44" wide)
- 5/8 yard green plaid
- 18" x 20" pillow form
- 20" square of batting

Cutting for the Pillow

- Cut 1: 3 1/2" x 20" strip, green print
- Cut 2: 2" x 22" strips, green print
- Cut 1: 20" square, yellow print, for the backing
- Cut 2: 2" x 20" strips, yellow print
- Cut 1: 3 1/2" x 22" strip, yellow print
- Cut 4: 6 1/2" squares, yellow print
- Cut 8: 3 1/2" x 18" strips, yellow print, for the ties
- Cut 1: 18 1/2" x 40 1/2" rectangle, green plaid, for the pillow cover
- Cut 1: 20" x 40" rectangle, muslin
- Cut 1: 20" square, muslin

Directions

- Fold the 18 1/2" x 40 1/2" green plaid rectangle in half, right side in, and stitch the raw edge with a 1/4" seam allowance, as shown.

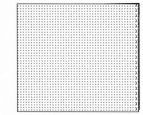

- Refold the unit, as shown, and stitch the remaining raw edges with a 1/4" seam allowance leaving an 8" opening in the center of one side.

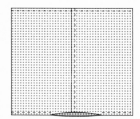

- Turn the unit right side out. Insert the pillow form and blindstitch the opening. Set the pillow aside.
- Stitch the 3 1/2" x 20" green print strip between two 2" x 20" yellow print strips to make a panel.
- Cut five 3 1/2" slices from the panel to make unit A.
- Stitch the 3 1/2" x 22" yellow print strip between two 2" x 22" green print strips to make a panel.
- Cut ten 2" slices from the panel to make unit B.
- Stitch a unit A between 2 unit B's to make a Puss-in-the-Corner block. Make 5.
- Referring to the pillow photo, lay out the Puss-in-the-Corner blocks and the 6 1/2" yellow print squares in 3 rows of 3.
- Stitch the blocks into rows. Join the rows.
- Layer in this manner: muslin, batting and pillow top, right side up, and quilt as desired.
- Fold a 3 1/2" x 18" yellow print strip, in half lengthwise, and stitch a 1/4" seam on one short side and one long side.
- Turn the strip right side out and press to make a tie. Make 8. Set them aside.
- Measure the size of the pillow top. Cut the 20" yellow print square to that measurement for the backing unit.
- Baste 4 of the ties in the seam allowance on the right side of the pillow top, aligning them as shown.

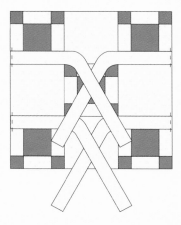

- Using their position as a guide, baste the remaining 4 ties in the seam allowance on the right side of the backing unit.
- Stitch the pillow top to the backing unit, right sides together, along one side without ties. Open and press the seam toward the backing.
- Measure the unit and trim the 20" x 40" muslin rectangle to that measurement.
- Place the pillow top/backing unit on the muslin rectangle, right sides together, and stitch along the 2 long sides, as shown, being careful not to catch the tails of the ties in the stitching.

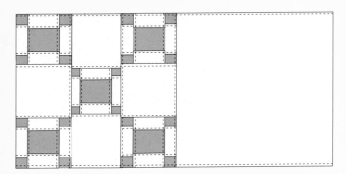

- Refold the unit so the right side of the backing unit is against the right side of the pillow top, and the unit forms a tube.
- Stitch around the unstitched edge of the tube until only a 10" opening is left on the lining side, as shown.

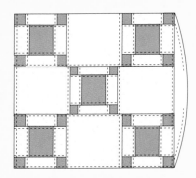

- Turn the pillow top through the opening and blindstitch the opening closed.
- Turn the pillow top so that the muslin lining is on the inside of the tube.
- Slide the pillow top over the pillow. Tie the ties to each other in bows.

Five Star Comfort (continued from page 14)

Assembly

- Lay out the Star blocks and Rail blocks in 3 rows of 3. Stitch the blocks into rows. Join the rows.

- Center and stitch a 4" x 56" tan with blue stripe strip to a 7 1/2" x 70" blue floral strip, right sides together, to make a pieced strip. Make 4.
- Center and stitch a pieced strip to each side of the quilt. Start and stop stitching 1/4" from the edges of the quilt top and backstitch.
- With the quilt top right side down, lay one border over the other. Draw a straight line at a 45° angle from the inner to the outer corners.

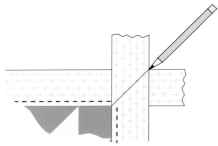

- Reverse the positions of the borders and mark another corner-to-corner line. With the borders right sides together, and the marked lines carefully matched, stitch from the inner seamline to the outer corner, backstitching at each end. Open the mitered seam to make sure it lies flat, then trim the excess fabric and press.
- Finish the quilt as described in the *General Directions* using the 2 1/2" x 44" tan with blue stripe strips for the binding.